M000287087

OUR FAMILY STORY

OUR FAMILY STORY

A journal to fill out together

PETE DUFFIELD

TarcherPerigee

tarcherperigee

An imprint of Penguin Random House LLC

penguinrandomhouse.com

Copyright © 2022 by Pete Duffield

Penguin supports copyright. Copyright fuels creativity,
encourages diverse voices, promotes free speech, and creates
a vibrant culture. Thank you for buying an authorized edition
of this book and for complying with copyright laws by not
reproducing, scanning, or distributing any part of it in
any form without permission. You are supporting writers and
allowing Penguin to continue to publish books for every reader.

TarcherPerigee with tp colophon is a
registered trademark of Penguin Random House LLC.

Most TarcherPerigee books are available at special quantity discounts for bulk
purchase for sales promotions, premiums, fund-raising, and educational needs.
Special books or book excerpts also can be created to fit specific needs. For
details, write: SpecialMarkets@penguinrandomhouse.com.

Library of Congress Control Number: 2022932784

ISBN 9780593421604

Printed in the United States of America

1st Printing

Book design by Pete Duffield

For Kellie, Poppy, Sophie, and Ryan,
who give my life meaning

THIS STORY BELONGS TO US:

Welcome

to OUR FAMILY STORY

Hello! I'm Pete of Kellie & Pete, and I draw silly illustrations of my family on the internet. I've found it's the perfect way to make a visual diary that celebrates the priceless time we spend together as a family.

I've created this book to inspire you to capture YOUR unique family story. It is a creative space for you to record precious memories and shared experiences, to explore your relationships, and to encourage you all to reflect on the quality time _you_ spend together.

Fill it with words, drawings, doodles, photos, and anything else you wish to use. Once completed, you will have a handwritten TIME CAPSULE of your family life, a keepsake treasured for years to come.

HOW TO USE THIS JOURNAL

Feel free to use this book in whichever way works best for your family. Flip to any random page, follow the prompts, and scribble down whatever inspires you. You could all sit down together to fill it out or take turns to write in it individually. It's recommended that every family member contributes to make it a collective effort, but that's completely up to you.

What you'll need

Be as creative and carefree as you want when filling out this book. ANYTHING GOES.

Pens, pencils, crayons, markers, paints— use whatever you feel :inspired: to use. Feel free to stick in as many photographs as you want, along with any little mementos and ephemera you find on your adventures.

Avoid being too precious. Just relax and have fun with it. ‿

Here's the

CAST of CHARACTERS

you'll see sprinkled throughout this book:

Kellie

Kellie is a super-organized and devoted mom, and the one who keeps the family running like clockwork. She's soft-spoken but has a hot temper.

Pete

Pete is a proud father whose family means everything to him. He's a kind introvert with a silly sense of humor and a penchant for daydreaming.

Poppy

Spirited and playful, Poppy is a ball of energy with a big imagination. She can be shy, but those close to her know how sweet and funny she is.

Your story starts here

Our Family

Draw all the members of your family here. Next to them write their ages, ♥LIKES and 💔DISLIKES, and anything else that makes them special.

Draw your trusty family pets and write their names, how old they are, and any quirky personality traits they have (e.g., occasionally eats shoes, insists on 3 a.m. zoomies...)

If you don't have any pets (or just want more), draw the pets you hope to have one day.

How long have you all lived here?

Things you LOVE about it:

What you'd like to change:

DRAW YOUR DREAM HOUSE

Where would it be? What would it look like?

GROWN-UPS

HOW you MET

Where did you meet?

When?

What were your first impressions of each other?

Draw or write about your first meeting:

Important People
IN YOUR LIVES

Draw the people who play a big part in your lives. This could be other family members, friends, teachers, colleagues, and neighbors.

GOALS

FOR THIS YEAR

- ☐ Complete this book! _____
- ☐ _____
- ☐ _____
- ☐ _____
- ☐ _____
- ☐ _____
- ☐ _____
- ☐ _____

Draw yourselves achieving one of your goals and write how it feels.

Write down what it is you love most about each other.

WHAT ARE YOUR FAVORITE THINGS ABOUT EACH OTHER?

Draw somewhere that holds a special place in your hearts.
It can be wherever you feel your happiest and most content.

TRACE YOUR HANDS

Use different colors for each hand and write the person's name on each. Add the fingernails too, if you like. Who has the longest? Who bites them?

CHECKLIST

- [ ] Face mask
- [ ] Manicure
- [ ] Foot soak
- [ ] Massage
- [ ] Pedicure
- [ ] Hot bath
- [ ] Candles
- [ ] Bathrobes
- [ ] Slippers
- [ ] Glass of wine or orange juice

Other things you like to do to unwind:

FEARS (AND) PHOBIAS

Circle the things that send shivers down your spine.

SPIDERS

TALKING ON THE PHONE

WASPS

SNAKES

SKELETONS

BATH TIME

COMMITMENT

VEGETABLES

FLYING

PUBLIC SPEAKING

DOGS

GHOSTS

HOMEWORK

THE DARK

HEIGHTS

BEING ALONE

ZOMBIES

DIRTY DISHES

BEING
EMBARRASSED

THUNDERSTORMS

Add some terrifying things of your own:

Draw yourselves as
SUPERHEROES
or even SUPERVILLAINS!

What are your SUPERPOWERS? Do you have any _weaknesses?_
What's your :TEAM: name?

Help Poppy finish this UNDERWATER scene.

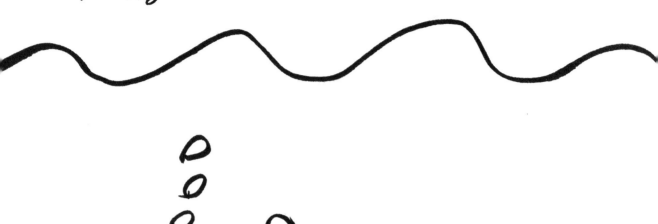

DRAW YOUR PAJAMAS HERE:

Cook Together

What are your favorite foods to cook?

FAVORITE CUISINES

- ☐ Thai
- ☐ Indian
- ☐ Chinese
- ☐ Barbecue
- ☐ Italian
- ☐ Mexican
- ☐ Japanese

Who's the **BEST CHEF** in the house?

Who's the worst?

Who's the fussiest eater?

Pass a lazy afternoon gazing up at the clouds in the sky. Draw the shapes you see in them.

Cloud Spotting

WHAT ARE YOUR ANNOYING HABITS?

Draw or write down the bad habits you have that drive each other crazy. You could add your own or do each other's.

Go for a WALK in NATURE

DATE:

LOCATION:

Draw or stick in a photo of the scenery here:

Draw 3 types of *leaves* you found:

Draw 3 *living things* you saw:

Who did you make it for?

What did you make?

What was their reaction?

BUY MORE PLANTS FOR YOUR HOME

☼ AND TRY TO KEEP THEM THRIVING ☼

Circle the plants you've managed to keep alive so far:

Snake

Rubber

Cactus

Spider

English ivy

Aloe vera

Peace lily

Succulent

Add any other plants you have here
(write any names you have for them too!)

SPIRIT
ANIMALS

If you could be any ANIMALS, which ones would you be and WHY? Draw animal versions of yourselves and write down any characteristics you share with them.

☆ YOUR FAMILY ☆
ACHIEVEMENTS

Fill these shelves with all of your proud achievements. They can be real trophies, medals, certificates, or made-up ones you want to award each other.

What are some other talents that each of you
is particularly proud of? Write or draw them here.

THINGS YOU WORRY ABOUT AT NIGHT

Write down any thoughts and worries that are on your mind when you're trying to fall asleep.

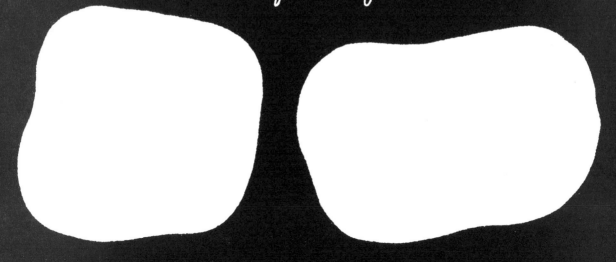

KIDS
Draw the
GROWN-UPS

Draw their HAPPY faces:

Draw their GRUMPY faces:

Draw how their HAIR looks when they wake up:

Draw them being chased by a <u>HUNGRY BEAR</u>:

Draw them riding a DINOSAUR:

YOUR FUTURE SELVES

Draw your family TEN years from now.

Write a letter to your future selves.

Dear Future Us,

Try to live in the moment.

MAKE HOMEMADE PIZZAS

What are all your FAVORITE toppings? Draw them on.

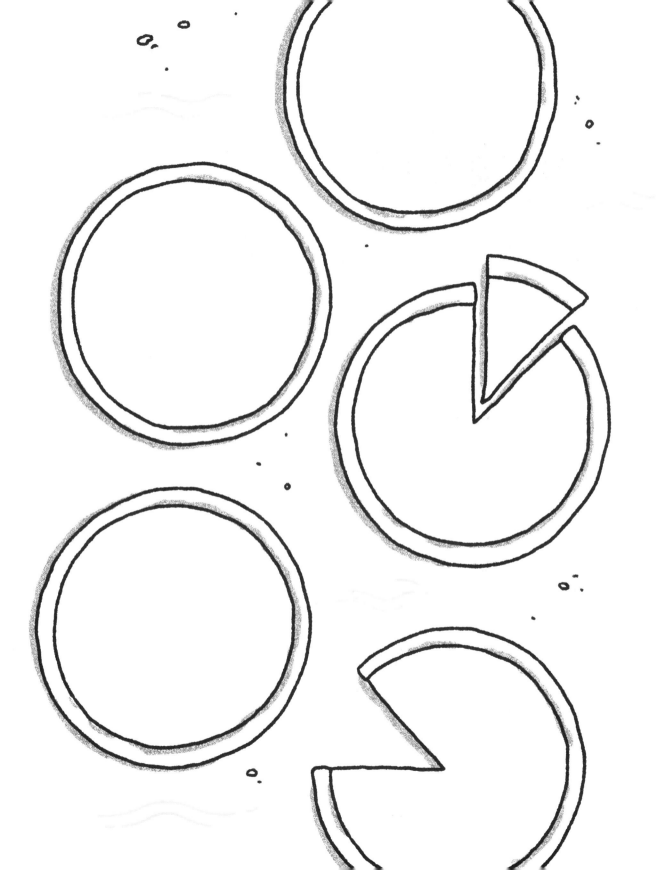

Beach Day

Take a family trip to the beach.

CHECKLIST

- [ ] Sunscreen
- [ ] Beach towels
- [ ] Collect shells
- [ ] Shades/sunglasses
- [ ] Build sandcastles
- [ ] Bury your legs in the sand
- [ ] A good book to read
- [ ] Overcrowded beach
- [ ] Hot sand burning your feet
- [ ] Buy ice cream (bonus points for eating it before it melts)
- [ ] One of you gets Sunburned

Draw some of the things that you saw and did.

BIRTHDAY PARTY
Play list

Don't be scared of
blank space. Fill it
however you like.

Spend 30 minutes
doing something
for your partner
that they LOVE ♡

MOVIE NIGHT

CHECKLIST

- ☐ Popcorn
- ☐ Comfy couch
- ☐ Cushions
- ☐ Snacks
- ☐ Soda
- ☐ Phones turned off
- ☐ PJs
- ☐ Blankets

What are your favorite movies?

YOUR DAILY ROUTINE

What time you usually wake up:

What you like for breakfast:

How you spend your time during the day:

In the evenings you:

For dinner you might have:

Bedtime is around:

Take a family Selfie

Print your selfie out and stick it here:

IF YOU HAD A TIME MACHINE

~~~ When and where would you travel? ~~~

Draw some of the people and places throughout history (or in the FUTURE) you'd like to visit:

SPACE

Use these pages for <u>anything</u> you like.

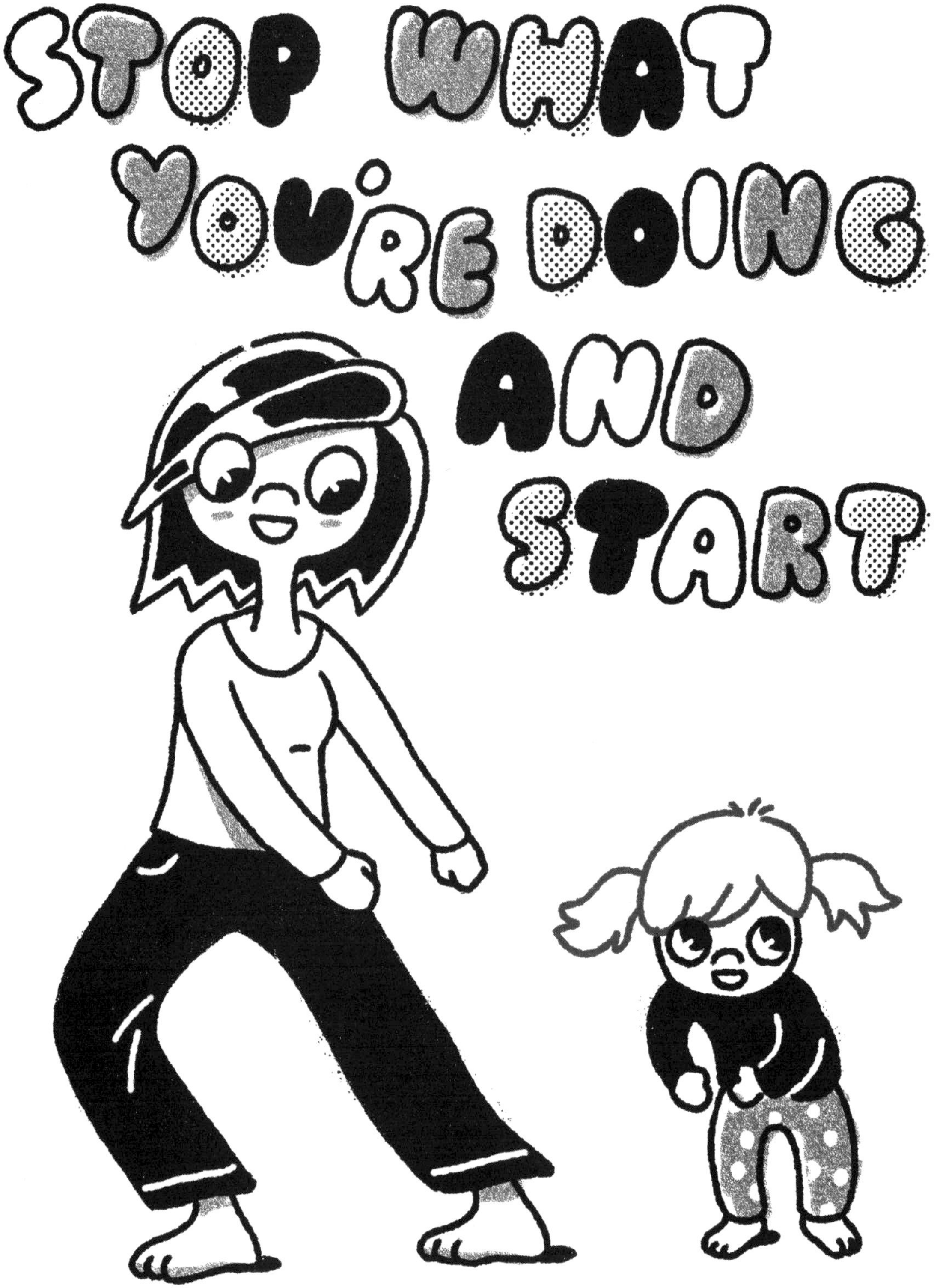
STOP WHAT YOU'RE DOING AND START

HOW DO YOU MAKE EACH OTHER

Smile?

What are the cute or funny things you say and do to make each other happy?

SLEEPING ARRANGEMENTS

(Daddy sleeping in Poppy's bed)

This is my safe place

It's too hot to cuddle—let's touch butts

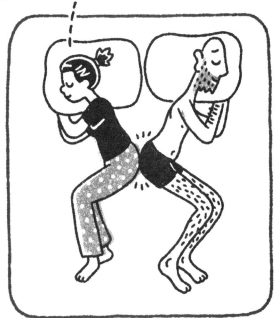

I call this "The Octopus"

Draw your family's favorite sleeping positions:
(Add any funny notes and details too!)

It's okay

to have

bad days

VACATION

Play list

WORD SEARCH

```
Z U Z H A U U P L Q L O E Y
Y S Z M W U T O G E T H E R
Q U S P R E C I O U S W S M
J J P J G W O D T K K W E E
F O P C H M W Y P C O F U M
Z A U X H O M E P N M J P O
E M V R O R M L Z S P I I R
T M J M N Z X O F D M R D I
N F R I S A Z V U A P Q D E
S X A N O B L E B W M O W S
T C P D Y J P S B J H I M U
O Q W F F A V O R I T E L M
R H L U V L P A G W I D F Y
Y R N L W L B P S Q B O R M
```

FAVORITE   TOGETHER   MEMORIES
JOURNAL   PRECIOUS   MINDFUL
STORY   HOME   LOVE   FAMILY

Kids Say the FUNNIEST THINGS

WRITE DOWN SOME OF THE HILARIOUS AND/OR RANDOM THINGS YOUR CHILDREN SAY.

FAMILY Vacations

Draw and describe the best places you've visited together.

If you could go anywhere as a family, where would you go? It could even be somewhere wild like OUTER SPACE 🪐

Who has the biggest sweet tooth?

FAMILY TRADITIONS

Use this space to write about all of the rituals, traditions, and quirky habits that make your family unique.

MAKE FUNNY FACES

DO SOME
BAKING

Spend some quality time together baking something delicious.

What did you make? Add your recipe here:

How did it taste? Will you make it again?

TRACE YOUR FEET

(or just your toes if your feet don't fit here)

You could use different colors for each foot and label each one. Bonus points if you draw the fluff between the toes.

CHECKLIST

- [ ] Carve a pumpkin
- [ ] Eat some candy
- [ ] ...Eat too much candy
- [ ] Play scary music
- [ ] Go trick-or-treating
- [ ] Watch a scary movie
- [ ] Get dressed up
- [ ] Bake Halloween treats
- [ ] Make fall crafts
- [ ] Play Halloween games

HALLOWEEN

Draw your costumes or something SPOOKY you baked or made.

Your Favorite TOYS

What are the toys you love to play with the most?

Include any names you have for them, what their personalities are, and describe the funny voices your parents do for them!

Have a FAMILY meal at a RESTAURANT

Where did you go?

What did you talk about?
Did you like what you ordered?

Draw what you
all had to eat.

What's on your MIND?

— GET SOME THINGS —
OFF YOUR CHEST

Things you're upset about:

Chores you need to get done:

Stuff you're excited for:

You're feeling anxious about:

The funniest thing that happened this week:

Write down some things you could do with your time instead of doomscrolling.

STOP SCROLLING AND PUT YOUR PHONE DOWN

Kellie
& Pete

SICK DAYS

What are the ways your family COMFORTS and CARES for one another when one of you is under the weather?

Fill these pages with any times you've been sick this year and how the family helped you through it.

What do you want to be when you GROW UP?

Ask your children what they want to be when they're older and get them to draw or write their answer here.

Slow down
and notice
the _little_
things

MAKE UP A
BEDTIME STORY

Using your IMAGINATION 🌈

SOME FANTASTICAL IDEAS TO GET YOU STARTED

- ☐ Witches
- ☐ Dragons
- ☐ Kings
- ☐ Magic
- ☐ Treasure
- ☐ A favorite toy
- ☐ A hidden forest
- ☐ Your own child
- ☐ Princesses
- ☐ Beanstalks
- ☐ "To be continued"
- ☐ Funny voices
- ☐ Fairies

write down your story here or in a separate notebook.

what did your child think of the story?

Help Poppy finish this OUTER SPACE scene.

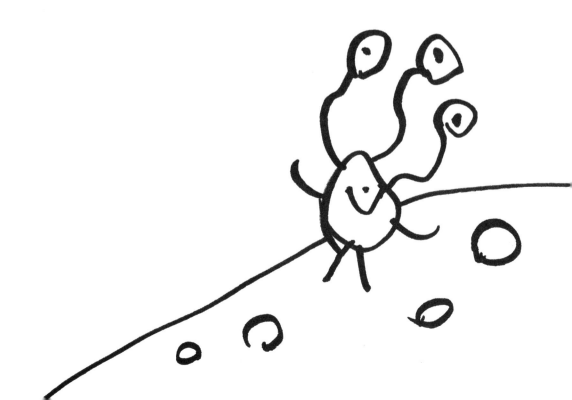

Can you find and circle the TEN differences between these two drawings?

Go for a PICNIC

Spend some quality time together relaxing in the sunshine.

Where you went:

What the weather was like:

WHAT TO PACK

- ☐ Blankets
- ☐ Sunscreen
- ☐ Trash bags
- ☐ Glasses/cups
- ☐ Thermos
- ☐ Plates and cutlery
- ☐ Ice packs
- ☐ Paper towels
- ☐ Shades/sunglasses

What are your favorite picnic foods?

FAMILY ARGUMENTS

Differences and disagreements are a natural and inevitable part of family life. Write about a recent dispute you've had and how you worked together to resolve it.

What was the argument about?

How was it resolved?

Do you still feel any resentment about what happened?

Is there anything you'd like to explain further or apologize for?

CAR JOURNEY

Play list

- ▶ _____
- ▶ _____
- ▶ _____
- ▶ _____
- ▶ _____
- ▶ _____
- ▶ _____

◄◄ ▶ ►►

Garden
SCAVENGER HUNT

Explore your backyard or neighborhood park and encourage your child to look closely to see what they can find. Looking through a child's eyes can also help you rediscover your own curiosity and sense of wonder.

THINGS TO LOOK OUT FOR

- ☐ Snail
- ☐ Beetle
- ☐ Slug
- ☐ Earthworm
- ☐ Butterfly
- ☐ Feather

- ☐ Spider
- ☐ Ant
- ☐ Fly
- ☐ Bee
- ☐ Dandelion
- ☐ Pine cone

- ☐ Ladybug
- ☐ Daisy
- ☐ Bird
- ☐ Frog
- ☐ Caterpillar
- ☐ Spider's web

Draw some of the things you found:

Send each other a cute
TEXT MESSAGE

Write what you sent in the bubbles below:

Go for a
CYCLE / SCOOTER RIDE

Get out in the fresh air and explore new places on a family adventure.

DATE:

LOCATION:

ADMIRE THE SCENERY

Stop and take a photo or draw a picture of the view.

Write about how the ride was:

Your
FAVORITE
OUTFITS

Show off your style (or lack of it) and draw your favorite clothes and accessories.

SPRING / SUMMER :

FALL/WINTER:

Draw some of your favorite videos on the internet:

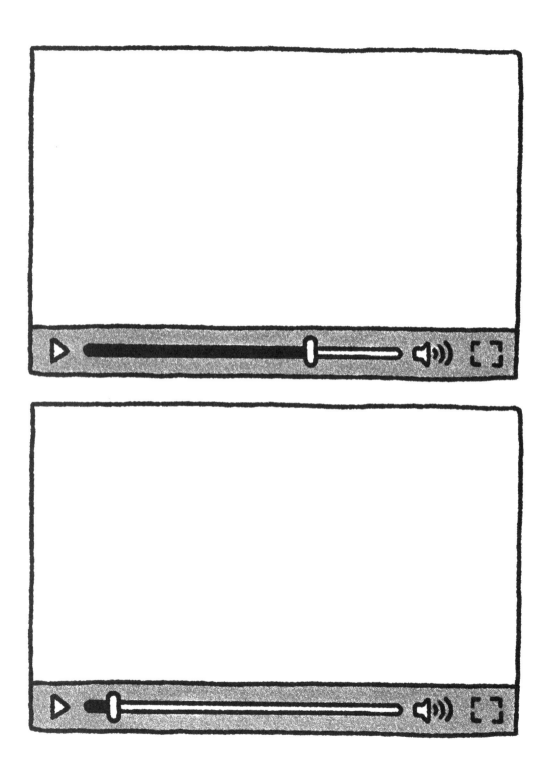

MAKE CHALK DRAWINGS ON THE SIDEWALK

Stick in a photo or re-create

YOUR MASTERPIECE

The WEEKEND

How do you like to spend time together as a FAMILY?

WINTER

CHECKLIST

- ☐ Go ice-skating
- ☐ Wrap presents
- ☐ Have a snowball fight
- ☐ Go sledding
- ☐ Cozy up by a warm fire
- ☐ Put up decorations
- ☐ Watch "Elf"
- ☐ Build a snowman
- ☐ Make snow angels
- ☐ Bake gingerbread men

Draw your favorite things about the winter season.

You're
PRECIOUS

MAKE SOMEONE A
NICE HOT DRINK

ABSOLUTELY ESSENTIAL EXTRAS

- ☐ Cookies to dunk
- ☐ Whipped cream
- ☐ Marshmallows
- ☐ Hot bath
- ☐ Favorite TV show
- ☐ Peace and quiet

Your favorite hot drinks:

Who makes the <u>BEST</u> hot drinks?

Peeeete, would you make me a tea?
I made my own but it didn't taste
as good because it wasn't made with
⋛LOVE⋚

Use this space to write about your most precious family memories.

Cherished Memories

FOODS on the WILL-NOT-EAT LIST

Circle the foods you don't want anywhere near your mouth.

CARROTS

FISH

MUSHROOMS

HAMBURGERS

BROCCOLI

TOMATOES

RAISINS

CHEESE

BRUSSELS SPROUTS

PEANUT BUTTER

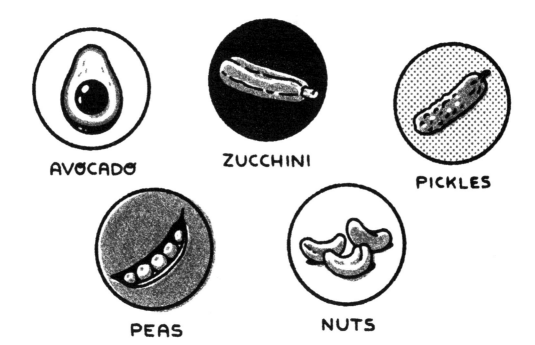

AVOCADO

ZUCCHINI

PICKLES

PEAS

NUTS

What others make your list?

MAKE TIME
TO HUG EACH
OTHER EVERY
SINGLE DAY

Go CAMPING

(Even if it's in your own backyard or home.)

DATE: | LOCATION:

THINGS YOU COULD DO

- ☐ Make a fire
- ☐ Sing songs
- ☐ Gaze at stars
- ☐ Go fishing
- ☐ Hunt for treasure

- ☐ Tell scary stories
- ☐ Toast marshmallows
- ☐ Play board games
- ☐ Make s'mores

Stick a photo or draw a picture of the view.

What are your favorite moments from the night?

TV SHOWS

Draw a scene featuring all of your favorite TV show characters.

Have some ME time

Having some quality time to yourself is an essential part of family life. How do _you_ like to spend time alone?

Write the things you've DISCOVERED
about your family from using this book:

What were your FAVORITE parts of this experience?
Did you learn anything :NEW: about yourselves?

ACKNOWLEDGMENTS

First and foremost, I would like to thank my partner, Kellie, without whom this book would never have been possible. You have been my muse from the moment I met you, and you continue to inspire me every single day. You tolerate my many moods with understanding and patience, and always make me laugh when I take myself too seriously. Thank you for being my best friend, and for giving me so much love and support while I was lost in my own head for months making this book.

Special thanks to my three beautiful children. You have given my life meaning and fulfillment beyond what I thought possible. Thank you for putting up with me obsessively talking about this book over the past few months, and for your boundless encouragement. I am truly blessed to be your father.

A huge thank you to my editor, Lauren, who helped shape my early incoherent scribblings into a finished book I'm so proud of. Your guidance and expertise were an immeasurable help throughout the process, and your ability to improve my work with every suggestion never failed to impress me.
It was an absolute pleasure to work with you.

Additionally, I owe an enormous debt of gratitude to Marian at TarcherPerigee for discovering my work and seeing the potential in it. Thank you for taking a chance on me; I will always remember it.

A big thank you to my boss, Dan, at Buffalo, whose encouragement and understanding enabled me to create this book. Your willingness to accommodate my needs throughout this project is massively appreciated.

Thank you to my mum, whose financial and emotional support while I worked on this book was vital. You're always there for me and help in any way you can, and that means the world to me.

Finally, a thank you to all my friends and colleagues who gave me advice and suggestions during the making of this book. Your insightful comments, constructive criticism, and the overriding belief you showed in me were constant sources of motivation.